BORN TO RULE

SHEPHERD'S ROD 2021

TERRY G. WITHERSPOON

ASCENDANCY
PUBLISHING

Born to Rule: Shepherd's Rod 2021
Published by Ascendancy Publishing

Contact Lasting Liberty Ministries:
PO Box #141913
3900 Teleport Blvd
Irving, TX 75014
www.lastingliberty.org

Scripture quotations marked (NKJV) are taken from the New King James Version®. Copyright © 1982 by Thomas Nelson. Used by permission. All rights reserved.
Scripture quotations marked (AMPC) are taken from the Amplified® Bible (AMPC), Copyright © 1954, 1958, 1962, 1964, 1965, 1987, 2015 by the Lockman Foundation 2015 Used by permission. www.Lockman.org
Scripture quotations marked (ESV) are from ESV® Bible (The Holy Bible, English Standard Version®), copyright © 2001 by Crossway, a publishing ministry of Good News Publishers. Used by permission. All rights reserved.
Scripture quotations marked (WEB) are from the World English Bible.

ISBN 978-0-9983923-3-2

Copyright © 2020 by Terry G. Witherspoon

All rights reserved. No part of this book may be reproduced or transmitted in any form or by any means, electronic, mechanical, including photocopying, recording, or by any information storage and retrieval systems, without written permission from the author.

Printed in the United States of America
2020

Some names have been changed to protect the privacy of individuals.

Background cardboard texture photo created by tirachard
- www.freepik.com
Key vector created by macrovector_official - www.freepik.com
Crown vector created by FreePik - www.freepik.com
Cover design, interior design, and editing by Kristen Witherspoon

TABLE OF CONTENTS

FOREWORD 7

CHAPTER 1 *Waves of Change* 11

CHAPTER 2 *No Dumb Dog* 15

CHAPTER 3 *Listen and Obey* 21

CHAPTER 4 *The Power of Words* 33

CHAPTER 5 *The Power of Unity* 45

CHAPTER 6 *The Power of Imagination* 55

CHAPTER 7 *He Will Give Us Rest* 77

CHAPTER 8 *Zion is Coming* 87

CHAPTER 9 *Rule or Be Ruled* 117

FOREWORD

I've known Brother Terry Witherspoon for many years now. He is a wonderful man of God. It is an honor for me to write this forward. Terry's Shepherd's Rod 2021 is titled ***Born to Rule***!

Within these prophetic pages you will quickly discover that Father God has chosen you and appointed you to rule and reign.

I recommend this book to you. Get your Bible and a paper and dig deep into these treasures of truth. Your life will be greatly enhanced.

Bobby Conner
Eagles View Ministries
www.bobbyconner.org

In Dedication To:
My wife, Renee, our children,
and daughter-in-love:
Jacob Witherspoon
Kristen Witherspoon
Joshua and Brittany Witherspoon

1

WAVES OF CHANGE

Sometime in 2014, after leading a series of meetings I found myself driving from Tennessee to Moravian Falls, North Carolina. It was a six hour drive each way and after arriving there, I felt led to locate the gravesite of Bob Jones who had passed away earlier that year.

Bob Jones was a very high-level prophet that was used in mighty ways by the Lord. I met Bob through my friend Bobby Conner who is also a very high-level prophet. Once I arrived at the gravesite I stood there reflecting on Bob's ministry and thanking the Lord for his life.

Suddenly I heard a loud humming sound coming from behind me. I turned and saw a very large hummingbird hovering over me. I've never seen such a large hummingbird. It zipped from one side to the next for a few seconds looking directly at me as though it was inspecting me. It then quickly flew into the trees until it was out of sight.

I thought it was very strange and so I sat on a concrete bench nearby to pray. I was soon overcome by a deep sleep. All I could do was lay back on the bench and then I went unconscious.

Sometime later I was awakened by a strong shaking sensation that seemed to move me from one side to the next. It literally felt as though I was experiencing an earthquake. I clearly remember the shaking was so violent that the pen I had in my shirt pocket shook loose until it fell out onto the ground.

I sat up on the bench somewhat dazed trying to collect my thoughts. I then picked my pen up from the ground and left.

The Lord had used Bob Jones for several years to receive the Shepherd's Rod for His people. I didn't realize at the time that the Lord was giving me prophetic signs that He wanted me to receive and write the Shepherd's Rod.

The Shepherd's Rod is a yearly time, during Yom Kippur also known as the Day of Atonement, when God will visit His prophets to review the condition of the sheep (see Ezekiel 20:37). He symbolically causes the sheep to pass under the rod of His Shepherd in order to inspect them. The Lord will also reveal some of the things to come in the future.

This current year, 2020, the Lord spoke to me in a dream and later by the Holy Spirit that I was to receive the coming year's Shepherd Rod (for 2021). So I drove, at the Lord's instruction, from the Dallas area to Moravian Falls, North Carolina.

I felt God telling me to go there for the coming Yom Kippur or Day of Atonement. After two days of driving I felt again that I was to go to the gravesite of Bob Jones.

And now six years later, I found myself standing and praying in the same spot. As I gazed at the gravesite I prayed and thanked the Lord for Bob's life.

Suddenly I looked at the ground which began to take on unusual physical characteristics. It instantly appeared to take on the shape and behavior of water. I could see the grass, dirt, and texture like normal ground but it undulated and moved as though it were literally waves of water. This lasted for a couple of minutes.

Luke 21:25-26 NKJV
(25) "And there will be signs in the sun, in the moon, and in the stars; and on the earth distress of nations, with perplexity, the sea and the waves roaring;

(26) men's hearts failing them from fear and
the expectation of those things which are
coming on the earth, for the powers of the
heavens will be shaken.

God's people need to know what we should be doing in these dark days. During the Day of Atonement, I felt led to Psalms 82. We can glean critical information about what God's people should be applying ourselves to. Take note of Psalms 82:5 below.

The foundations of the earth are unstable because wickedness rules.

There is a shaking coming to not only the earth but also the heavens (see Hebrews 2:25-26). God is allowing this shaking to remove the middle ground. People will be forced to choose which side to jump to as the middle ground collapses.

These are exciting times for God's people. He is releasing more to us and positioning us to rule.

Psalms 82:5 NKJV
(5) They do not know, nor do they
understand; They walk about in darkness;
All the foundations of the earth are unstable.

2

NO DUMB DOG

> Surely the Lord GOD does nothing,
> Unless He reveals His secret
> to His servants the prophets.
> – Amos 3:7 (NKJV)

God has always revealed His plans to his servants the prophets and there is no indication in Scripture that God has stopped doing this.

I drove two days from the Dallas area to Moravian Falls, North Carolina and when I got there rented a cabin owned by a very nice couple named Linda and Rob. They were telling me about the place as their dog came running up to greet me.

Rob said, "You must like animals. My dog, Dorado, can always tell when someone likes animals. He's always very friendly to those kinds of people." Dorado was a large Labrador and Belgian Shepherd mix. He had some gray around the whiskers displaying the wisdom he had earned.

NO DUMB DOG

I reached down to pet Dorado and then scratched his back while visiting with his owners. If I didn't know better, I would swear that Dorado was smiling at me as he looked up.

A couple of hours later, I was walking to the communal restrooms when I saw Dorado looking at me from one of the other cabins. He suddenly started barking and then aggressively charged toward me stopping right in front of me. I tried to calm him down by saying his name but he just kept aggressively barking like crazy. Rob frantically yelled at him several times until Dorado finally stopped barking and returned to him.

I was struck by how different Dorado's behavior was toward me since he had been so warm and friendly earlier. It definitely seemed out of the ordinary and prophetic.

Once I got back into the cabin I could look out the window and see Dorado standing about 35 yards away. I began to whisper under my breath, "You're a very bad dog. Why would you bark at me like that when you were so friendly before?"

Then strangely enough, Dorado turned his head to the left, looked over his shoulder directly at me, and made eye contact with me! I was stunned as I stood gazing out the window.

I then whispered, "You must be a good dog now and sit." Dorado instantly sat down! There is no way Dorado was hearing me in the natural. Whatever was happening was in the spirit realm and must have some prophetic meaning.

Two days later I was preparing to go home after spending the Day of Atonement in prayer and ministering to the Lord. I knew my prophet friend, Bobby Conner, was not far away and so I contacted him. We spoke by phone and he told me he was in the process of writing the Shepherd's Rod.

I told Bobby that the Lord had sent me to Moravian Falls at the last minute for the Day of Atonement. Bobby then said, "Obedience is better than sacrifice. In fact, sometimes the obedience is the sacrifice."

He asked if I had received anything from the Lord? I responded by saying that I had received some things from Him.

Bobby then began praying that we would release a sure word from the Lord to His people. Bobby quoted Isaiah 56:10, saying that we don't want to be like a watchdog that won't bark. He continued saying that we must declare all that the Lord has said and not leave anything out.

NO DUMB DOG

Isaiah 56:10-12 NKJV

(10) His watchmen are blind, They are all ignorant; They are all dumb dogs, They cannot bark; Sleeping, lying down, loving to slumber.

(11) Yes, they are greedy dogs Which never have enough. And they are shepherds Who cannot understand; They all look to their own way, Every one for his own gain, From his own territory.

(12) "Come," one says, "I will bring wine, And we will fill ourselves with intoxicating drink; Tomorrow will be as today, And much more abundant."

It's my heart's desire to do exactly that. I have never been asked to receive the Shepherd's Rod by the Lord before. I fully intend to do the best I can do with the help of the Holy Spirit in saying exactly what God has said to me.

We are living in days when it is critical for God's people to have clear direction from Him. We need to have men and women so fully yielded to the Person of the Holy Spirit that they can speak as oracles of the living God (see 1 Peter 4:11).

Our country is in trouble today. We have fallen

so far from our founding principles. Our nation has rejected God and His standards for living. Some of the sins that have become rampant during recent generations include: abortion, homosexuality, violence, racism, socialism (covetousness), perversion of marriage, perversion of the family unit, drug and alcohol addiction, pornography, rebellion, theft, etc.

The world or lost people are not to blame for the downward spiral of our nation. Unsaved people are slaves to the devil and sin. The church is at fault. Specifically, too many shepherds in the church have failed.

The watchmen have too often failed to call out and sound the alarm. Many church leaders have compromised God's standards and failed to preach God's message of holiness. They were more concerned about pleasing people than God. Some were more concerned with building their own kingdom instead of establishing the Lord's.

Our country was being overrun by demonic forces and too few of God's leaders were willing to sound the alarm. God compares these leaders to watch dogs that can't bark.

God will restore the fear of the Lord and raise up a people that fear nothing or no one except Him (see

Revelation 21:8, Deuteronomy 4:10, and Jeremiah 32:39).

God is stirring the hearts of many people today with a desire and conviction to return to Him. He will raise up shepherds that reflect His heart.

> **Jeremiah 3:15 AMPC**
> And I will give you [spiritual] shepherds after My own heart [in the final time], who will feed you with knowledge and understanding and judgment.

It's time for many shepherds to repent for not sounding the alarm. We must repent for seeking our own ways and for not being salt and light. We must repent for compromising His word. We must repent for not seeking God's face and for not keeping Him as our first love.

God will quickly forgive and restore.

> **Zechariah 9:12 ESV**
> Return to your stronghold, O prisoners of hope; today I declare that I will restore to you double.

3

LISTEN AND OBEY

I heard the Lord say,
"Terry, listen to me. My people
will escape these hard times as they
listen to Me and obey Me in faith.

They will be led to a higher place of
authority in Me that will allow Me to rule
in and through them.

They will soon discover the vast difference
between the vain and the valuable."

LISTEN AND OBEY

Shortly after moving from West Texas to the Dallas area we hosted a meeting called '*Take the Land*' with Bobby Conner. A few days later, my wife and I were having coffee and getting ready for the day.

Suddenly something manifested and then fell onto the tile floor a couple of feet from my wife. It made a very loud noise as it hit the floor. I quickly went to see what it was. A quarter had fallen out of thin air onto the floor! I sent a photo of it to Bobby and he responded, "Change is in the air."

There is no question that major changes are occurring throughout the world. We are seeing unprecedented shifts in every area of life. God has declared that there would be a shaking experienced by the world (see Hebrews 12:22-29). God intends to shake everything that can be shaken so that His kingdom will be established.

Many today have directed their faith toward everything except God. Many people trust in their government, their education, their wealth, or demonic religions.

God is allowing a shaking to occur to expose false gods and misplaced trust. The coming days will be the best of times and the worst of times. The best of days for people that place their trust in the Lord Jesus.

LISTEN AND OBEY

The coming days will be the worst for those who refuse His call.

Hebrews 12:25-29 NKJV
(25) See that you do not refuse Him who speaks. For if they did not escape who refused Him who spoke on earth, much more shall we not escape if we turn away from Him who speaks from heaven,

(26) whose voice then shook the earth; but now He has promised, saying, "YET ONCE MORE I SHAKE NOT ONLY THE EARTH, BUT ALSO HEAVEN."

(27) Now this, "YET ONCE MORE," indicates the removal of those things that are being shaken, as of things that are made, that the things which cannot be shaken may remain.

(28) Therefore, since we are receiving a kingdom which cannot be shaken, let us have grace, by which we may serve God acceptably with reverence and godly fear.

(29) For our God is a consuming fire.

The shaking that is coming is going to make room for something greater. In the previous scripture Hebrews 12:26, Paul quoted the prophet Haggai.

LISTEN AND OBEY

Haggai 2:6-9 ESV

(6) For thus says the LORD of hosts: Yet once more, in a little while, I will shake the heavens and the earth and the sea and the dry land.

(7) And I will shake all nations, so that the treasures of all nations shall come in, and I will fill this house with glory, says the LORD of hosts.

(8) The silver is mine, and the gold is mine, declares the LORD of hosts.

(9) The latter glory of this house shall be greater than the former, says the LORD of hosts. And in this place I will give peace, declares the LORD of hosts.'"

God is preparing a people that will carry His greater glory on the earth. We are the latter temple being built up to carry His greater glory. We are truly receiving a kingdom that cannot be shaken. We dare not refuse Him who speaks from Heaven (see Hebrews 12:25).

We must hear the Lord and obey Him now more than ever before. If He has commanded us to hear and obey He must be offering the ability to do both. We must accept His offer to help us hear Him.

If you have accepted Jesus as your Lord and Savior then that is proof that you can hear Him.

LISTEN AND OBEY

John 6:44 NKJV
No one can come to Me unless the Father who sent Me draws him; and I will raise him up at the last day.

The first step in hearing our Lord is to believe we can hear Him. Jesus said we can hear Him and that we will follow Him. Everything is received by faith in the Kingdom of God. Only believe.

John 10:27 NKJV
My sheep hear My voice, and I know them, and they follow Me.

The next step to hearing the Lord is to draw near to Him. He has promised to draw near to us if we will draw near to Him.

James 4:8 WEB
Draw near to God, and he will draw near to you. Cleanse your hands, you sinners; and purify your hearts, you double-minded.

We must spend time in His word with a heart full of expectation that He will speak to us through His written word.

We must listen for Him if we're going to hear Him.

LISTEN AND OBEY

We must be willing to daily spend time with Him and listening for Him in prayer.

Obeying the Lord expresses love to Him. We don't obey Him in order to be righteous but because we love Him. And we obey Him because He has freed us to be free.

> **John 14:15 NKJV**
> If you love Me, keep My commandments.

> **1 John 5:2-3 WEB**
> (2) By this we know that we love the children of God, when we love God and keep his commandments.
>
> (3) For this is loving God, that we keep his commandments. His commandments are not grievous.

God will guide us into blessings and protection as we hear and obey Him. The following verses provide incredible promises for those who hear and obey.

> **John 14:23 NKJV**
> Jesus answered and said to him, "If anyone loves Me, he will keep My word; and My

LISTEN AND OBEY

Father will love him, and We will come to him and make Our home with him.

Deuteronomy 28:1-10 ESV

(1) "And if you faithfully obey the voice of the LORD your God, being careful to do all his commandments that I command you today, the LORD your God will set you high above all the nations of the earth.

(2) And all these blessings shall come upon you and overtake you, if you obey the voice of the LORD your God.

(3) Blessed shall you be in the city, and blessed shall you be in the field.

(4) Blessed shall be the fruit of your womb and the fruit of your ground and the fruit of your cattle, the increase of your herds and the young of your flock.

(5) Blessed shall be your basket and your kneading bowl.

(6) Blessed shall you be when you come in, and blessed shall you be when you go out.

(7) "The LORD will cause your enemies who rise against you to be defeated before you. They shall come out against you one way and flee before you seven ways.

(8) The LORD will command the blessing on you in your barns and in all that you undertake. And he will bless you in the land that the LORD your God is giving you.

(9) The LORD will establish you as a people holy to himself, as he has sworn to you, if you keep the commandments of the LORD your God and walk in his ways.

(10) And all the peoples of the earth shall see that you are called by the name of the LORD, and they shall be afraid of you.

God will also lift us to a higher place of authority as we hear and obey Him. As we humble ourselves before the Lord—He will lift us up.

1 Peter 5:6-7 AMPC
(6) Therefore humble yourselves [demote, lower yourselves in your own estimation] under the mighty hand of God, that in due time He may exalt you,

(7) Casting the whole of your care [all your anxieties, all your worries, all your concerns, once and for all] on Him, for He cares for you affectionately and cares about you watchfully.

LISTEN AND OBEY

> **Isaiah 66:1-2 ESV**
> (1) Thus says the LORD: "Heaven is my throne, and the earth is my footstool; what is the house that you would build for me, and what is the place of my rest?
>
> (2) All these things my hand has made, and so all these things came to be, declares the LORD. But this is the one to whom I will look: he who is humble and contrite in spirit and trembles at my word.

Jesus walked a sinless holy life as "Son of Man" on the earth. One thing that Jesus demonstrated was meekness. Meekness expressed a total dependence on His Father in Heaven for everything.

> **Matthew 11:29 AMPC**
> Take My yoke upon you and learn of Me, for I am gentle (meek) and humble (lowly) in heart, and you will find rest (relief and ease and refreshment and recreation and blessed quiet) for your souls.

> **Matthew 5:5 ESV**
> Blessed are the meek, for they shall inherit the earth.

Jesus said He didn't do the works but the Father

did the works through Him. Jesus said He only spoke what the Father told Him to speak. And He only did what He saw the Father do.

John 5:19 NKJV
Then Jesus answered and said to them, "Most assuredly, I say to you, the Son can do nothing of Himself, but what He sees the Father do; for whatever He does, the Son also does in like manner.

John 12:49 NKJV
For I have not spoken on My own authority; but the Father who sent Me gave Me a command, what I should say and what I should speak.

Jesus said that we can do nothing without Him. The word "nothing" is all exclusive. Nothing can be done without Jesus—but with Him all things can be done.

John 15:5 NKJV
"I am the vine, you are the branches. He who abides in Me, and I in him, bears much fruit; for without Me you can do nothing…"

Philippians 4:13 NKJV
I can do all things through Christ who strengthens me.

LISTEN AND OBEY

If we are fully yielded to Jesus and follow Him we will become synchronized with Him. To become one with Jesus will produce His life in us.

To only say what the Lord says and to only do what He is doing is the ultimate definition of Holiness.

> **John 17:20-23 ESV**
> (20) "I do not ask for these only, but also for those who will believe in me through their word,
>
> (21) that they may all be one, just as you, Father, are in me, and I in you, that they also may be in us, so that the world may believe that you have sent me.
>
> (22) The glory that you have given me I have given to them, that they may be one even as we are one,
>
> (23) I in them and you in me, that they may become perfectly one, so that the world may know that you sent me and loved them even as you loved me.

Being one with Jesus will result in an overcoming life. This overcoming life will result in our being seated with Him. This results in great authority and makes a way for Him to rule through us.

L I S T E N A N D O B E Y

Revelation 3:19-22 NKJV

(19) As many as I love, I rebuke and chasten. Therefore be zealous and repent.

(20) Behold, I stand at the door and knock. If anyone hears My voice and opens the door, I will come in to him and dine with him, and he with Me.

(21) To him who overcomes I will grant to sit with Me on My throne, as I also overcame and sat down with My Father on His throne.

(22) "He who has an ear, let him hear what the Spirit says to the churches."

Ephesians 2:6 AMPC

And He raised us up together with Him and made us sit down together [giving us joint seating with Him] in the heavenly sphere [by virtue of our being] in Christ Jesus (the Messiah, the Anointed One).

4

THE POWER OF WORDS

I then heard the Lord say,
"I'm delegating more power to words spoken in Me by faith. They will lift heavy objects by their words."

I asked, "What do you mean?"

He said, "They will learn how to do work the way I do work. By my voice/words.

There is a vast difference between old vain religion and a living faith in and through Me.

You can teach them The Power of Words."

THE POWER OF WORDS

There is an account of Jesus healing and teaching found in Matthew 12:22-37. It starts with people bringing a demon-possessed man that was blind and mute. Jesus healed the man and the multitudes were amazed.

But the religious leaders accused Jesus of healing the man by the power of the devil. Jesus pointed out to them that a house divided could not stand. In other words, it would make no sense for the devil to work against himself.

Jesus then gave a stern warning to anyone attributing the work of the Holy Spirit to the devil. Jesus said, "Anyone who speaks a word against the Son of Man, it will be forgiven him; but whoever speaks against the Holy Spirit, it will not be forgiven him, either in this age or in the age to come" (see Matthew 12:32 NKJV).

Jesus warned them about how important it was for good things to come out of their mouths. He also warned them that if bad things are in their hearts, then bad things would come out of their mouths (see Matthew 12:33-37).

Take note in Matthew 12:36-37 where Jesus said, "But I say to you that for every idle word men may speak, they will give account of it in the day of judgment. For by your words you will be justified, and by your words you will be condemned."

These are very sobering comments from our Lord regarding the words we use. Notice the word "*idle*" in verse 36. The original Greek word is "argos" which means: "*inactive, that is, unemployed; (by implication) lazy, useless: - barren, idle, slow*" (see Thayer's Greek Definitions).

This literally means that our words should be actively employed to do work and useful regarding the Kingdom of God! We really need a deeper appreciation for the power of our words.

Matthew 12:33-37 NKJV
(33) "Either make the tree good and its fruit good, or else make the tree bad and its fruit bad; for a tree is known by its fruit.

(34) Brood of vipers! How can you, being evil, speak good things? For out of the abundance of the heart the mouth speaks.

(35) A good man out of the good treasure of his heart brings forth good things, and an evil man out of the evil treasure brings forth evil things.

(36) But I say to you that for every idle word men may speak, they will give account of it in the day of judgment.

THE POWER OF WORDS

(37) For by your words you will be justified, and by your words you will be condemned."

In Matthew 16:17-19, the Lord congratulates Peter for getting the revelation that He was the Christ. Jesus goes on to say that He would build His Church on that revelation.

Then Jesus gives them the keys to the Kingdom! He tells them that whatever they bind on earth will be bound by Heaven. And whatever they loose on earth will be loosed by Heaven.

Matthew 16:17-19 NKJV

(17) Jesus answered and said to him, "Blessed are you, Simon Bar-Jonah, for flesh and blood has not revealed this to you, but My Father who is in heaven.

(18) And I also say to you that you are Peter, and on this rock I will build My church, and the gates of Hades shall not prevail against it.

(19) And I will give you the keys of the kingdom of heaven, and whatever you bind on earth will be bound in heaven, and whatever you loose on earth will be loosed in heaven."

Can you believe that Jesus has given us the keys

to the Kingdom (see Luke 12:32)? Keys are used for locking and unlocking. And the gates of Hades, the devil, will not prevail against it. Notice we are on offense and the devil is on defense.

How do we bind and loose? Take a look at Mark 11:12-24. Jesus and the disciples were walking by a fig tree that He had cursed the previous day. Peter was shocked and pointed out the withered fig tree to Jesus.

> **Mark 11:20-23 NKJV**
> (20) Now in the morning, as they passed by, they saw the fig tree dried up from the roots.
>
> (21) And Peter, remembering, said to Him, "Rabbi, look! The fig tree which You cursed has withered away."
>
> (22) So Jesus answered and said to them, "Have faith in God.
>
> (23) For assuredly, I say to you, whoever says to this mountain, 'Be removed and be cast into the sea,' and does not doubt in his heart, but believes that those things he says will be done, he will have whatever he says.

Jesus said they should have faith in God. He then said, "For assuredly, I say to you, whoever says to this mountain, 'Be removed and be cast into the sea,' and does not doubt in his heart, but believes that those things he says will be done, he will have whatever he says" (see Mark 11:23).

Jesus said,
"… have faith in God."
"… whoever SAYS to this mountain."
"… and does not doubt."
"… will have whatever he SAYS."

Again notice Jesus gave two conditions necessary for moving mountains or doing the impossible. Believe and speak. We bind and loose with our words. God has invested tremendous power in our tongues!

Proverbs 18:20-21 ESV
(20) From the fruit of a man's mouth his stomach is satisfied; he is satisfied by the yield of his lips.

(21) Death and life are in the power of the tongue, and those who love it will eat its fruits.

It really matters what we believe and say about God. Jesus taught a parable recorded in Luke 19:11-27. In the parable, a nobleman went to a far country to

THE POWER OF WORDS

receive for himself a kingdom and then to return. So he hired ten servants and gave them each 10 minas (currency). He instructed them to do business until he returned.

Some of the servants declared they would not let that nobleman rule over them. Then the nobleman returned and demanded an accounting of what each servant had gained from his investment.

The first two servants had gained 10 additional minas. The master commended them and then increased the amount of territory they would reign over.

Then the master asked the third servant what he had gained. The third servant said, "Master, here is your mina, which I have kept put away in a handkerchief. For I feared you, because you are an austere man. You collect what you did not deposit, and reap what you did not sow" (see Luke 19:20-21).

The nobleman then said to the servant, "Out of your own mouth I will judge you, you wicked servant. You knew that I was an austere man, collecting what I did not deposit and reaping what I did not sow" (see Luke 19:22).

Consider the Amplified Classic version for Luke 19:21 for those comments:

THE POWER OF WORDS

Luke 19:21 AMPC
For I was [constantly] afraid of you, because you are a stern (hard, severe) man; you pick up what you did not lay down, and you reap what you did not sow.

The servant said the nobleman was a stern, hard, or severe man. The servant was blaming the nobleman for his own inaction due to his own fear or unbelief. The nobleman then used the very words that came out of the servant's mouth as judgment against him.

We can see in this parable that what we say about God and His kingdom matters. We can also see that the Lord is expecting an increase in the things He has invested in us.

We are supposed to be doing business till He comes. We must not allow fear or unbelief to paralyze us into inaction. Our words are not supposed to be "idle."

The Lord Jesus has given us the keys to the kingdom. Keys are used to lock or unlock. He has sovereignly delegated great power and authority to us!

We must first draw near to Him in our hearts so that good things can come out of our mouths.

Isaiah 29:13-14 WEB
(13) The Lord said, "Because this people draws near with their mouth and honors

me with their lips, but they have removed their heart far from me, and their fear of me is a commandment of men which has been taught;

(14) therefore, behold, I will proceed to do a marvelous work among this people, even a marvelous work and a wonder; and the wisdom of their wise men will perish, and the understanding of their prudent men will be hidden."

Jesus has given us the power to bind and loose. This is how our Father "does heavy lifting." God will have a people that reflects Him on the earth. It's time for God's people to make our words active and productive in establishing our Father's kingdom on the earth. It's time to bind the devil and to loose Heaven's blessings on the earth. It's time to believe and to speak (see 2 Corinthians 4:13).

We were created to reflect our Father and to have dominion over every created thing on earth (see Genesis 1:26). Our Heavenly Father created everything into existence by speaking. He said, "Let there be" (see Genesis 1). We were created to reflect the image of our Heavenly Father.

Before Adam fell in sin he helped his Heavenly

THE POWER OF WORDS

Father create by using the words he spoke. There is an account during creation when God called the animals to march in front of Adam and then God sat back to see what Adam would call them.

> **Genesis 2:19 AMPC**
> And out of the ground the Lord God formed every [wild] beast and living creature of the field and every bird of the air and brought them to Adam to see what he would call them; and whatever Adam called every living creature, that was its name.

Whatever Adam called each animal was its name.

Adam was proclaiming what the characteristics and traits of each animal species would be like. For instance, the canine (dog) species is very different in characteristics and traits than the feline (cat) species. In Genesis 2:19 the word "*name*" in the original language means traits, reputation, or character. I believe Adam proclaimed with his mouth what each animal species' traits or "*name*" would be.

Adam co-labored with his Father during creation. We will co-labor with our Father in forging and restoring the world we live in now.

THE POWER OF WORDS

Psalms 115:14-16 AMPC
(14) May the Lord give you increase more and more, you and your children.

(15) May you be blessed of the Lord, Who made heaven and earth!

(16) The heavens are the Lord's heavens, but the earth has He given to the children of men.

Isaiah 58:12-14 AMPC
(12) And your ancient ruins shall be rebuilt; you shall raise up the foundations of [buildings that have laid waste for] many generations; and you shall be called Repairer of the Breach, Restorer of Streets to Dwell In.

(13) If you turn away your foot from [traveling unduly on] the Sabbath, from doing your own pleasure on My holy day, and call the Sabbath a [spiritual] delight, the holy day of the Lord honorable, and honor Him and it, not going your own way or seeking or finding your own pleasure or speaking with your own [idle] words,

(14) Then will you delight yourself in the Lord, and I will make you to ride on the high places of the earth, and I will feed you with the heritage [promised for you] of Jacob your father; for the mouth of the Lord has spoken it.

5

THE POWER OF UNITY

The Lord then said,
"You can teach them
The Power of Unity."

THE POWER OF UNITY

In the natural realm there are natural laws that are well known. Gravity is a natural law that produces predictable results. In a similar way, unity contains spiritual principles that produce predictable results as well.

The account of the Tower of Babel, in Genesis 11:1-9, illustrates the power of unity. At that time in history mankind spoke one language and one speech. This unified people decided to build a city and a tower whose top would reach the heavens.

They said, "Come, let us build ourselves a city, and a tower whose top is in the heavens; let us make a name for ourselves, lest we be scattered abroad over the face of the whole earth" (see Genesis 11: 4 NKJV).

Then the Lord came down to look at what they had built. "And the LORD said, 'Indeed the people are one and they all have one language, and this is what they begin to do; now nothing that they propose to do will be withheld from them'" (see Genesis 11:6).

God noted the unity of the people and literally said that nothing they imagine to do can be withheld from them! This is an astonishing truth regarding the power of unity from the mouth of God.

However, the people were trying to build their own name and following their own plans to reach the heavens. God had a better plan for mankind so He decided to go down and scatter the people by confusing their language. This ended the rebellious unity and dispersed the people to various tribes around the earth.

We can see God's plan regarding unity in Acts 2:1-6. After the crucifixion, the followers of Jesus had gathered to wait in Jerusalem as the Lord had previously instructed them (see Luke 24:49).

Verse 1 says that when the Day of Pentecost had come they were in one place and in one accord. In the name of Jesus, they were in one place and in unity of purpose.

Then the Power and Presence of God came like a mighty rushing wind. The fire of God came upon and in everyone there. The Holy Spirit moved through the people and they supernaturally spoke in other tongues.

There were Jews and devout men living there from "every nation under heaven" (see Acts 2:5). But when God showed up these people could understand each other even though they spoke different languages. It's as though God reversed what happened at the Tower of Babel.

God was now building unity in His name and

according to His plan that would reach Heaven.

Acts 2:1-6 ESV
(1) When the day of Pentecost arrived, they were all together in one place.

(2) And suddenly there came from heaven a sound like a mighty rushing wind, and it filled the entire house where they were sitting.

(3) And divided tongues as of fire appeared to them and rested on each one of them.

(4) And they were all filled with the Holy Spirit and began to speak in other tongues as the Spirit gave them utterance.

(5) Now there were dwelling in Jerusalem Jews, devout men from every nation under heaven.

(6) And at this sound the multitude came together, and they were bewildered, because each one was hearing them speak in his own language.

Ephesians 4:3 AMPC
Be eager and strive earnestly to guard and keep the harmony and oneness of [and produced by] the Spirit in the binding power of peace.

THE POWER OF UNITY

Since the day of Pentecost until now God has been building something in His name by the powerful Person of the Holy Spirit.

Unity is one of the key ingredients produced by the Holy Spirit that will release greater power and authority for God's people in the coming days.

As God's people yield to His Holy Spirit and follow Him there will be a supernatural bond that increases God's Presence among His people. God will increasingly do the impossible through His people as they walk in unity with each other and with His Presence.

As represented by the Tower of Babel account, nothing will be withheld from God's people as they walk in this unity and are yielded to His purposes.

In 1 Corinthians 6:19, the Apostle Paul wrote that our bodies are the temple of the Holy Spirit. As believers, God dwells in each of us!

Peter compared Jesus to a living stone. And then Peter said that we also are like living stones which are being built up together as a spiritual house (see 1 Peter 2:4-5).

Likewise Paul said in Ephesians 2:18–22 that we are all growing together and being fitted into a dwelling place of God in the Spirit!

THE POWER OF UNITY

Ephesians 2:18-22 ESV
(18) For through him we both have access in one Spirit to the Father.

(19) So then you are no longer strangers and aliens, but you are fellow citizens with the saints and members of the household of God,

(20) built on the foundation of the apostles and prophets, Christ Jesus himself being the cornerstone,

(21) in whom the whole structure, being joined together, grows into a holy temple in the Lord.

(22) In him you also are being built together into a dwelling place for God by the Spirit.

Unlike the Tower of Babel, this spiritual building that God is building is being promoted and enabled by His powerful Holy Spirit. Instead of scattering the people because of disobedience God is building unity by His Spirit. As God's people yield to His purposes nothing will be withheld from them!

One of the Pharisees came to Jesus in the Gospel of Mark and asked Him what was the greatest commandment. Jesus answered in Mark 12:29-30.

He said, "The first of all the commandments is:

'HEAR, O ISRAEL, THE LORD OUR GOD, THE LORD IS ONE. AND YOU SHALL LOVE THE LORD YOUR GOD WITH ALL YOUR HEART, WITH ALL YOUR SOUL, WITH ALL YOUR MIND, AND WITH ALL YOUR STRENGTH.' This is the first commandment."

In verse 29 Jesus said, "'HEAR, O ISRAEL, THE LORD OUR GOD, THE LORD IS ONE.'" This phrase can be interpreted as meaning that God is supreme and number one above all.

However, it can also be interpreted as meaning that the Lord is one with Himself. The Father, the Son, and the Holy Spirit are in perfect unity.

Jesus prayed that His followers would be one even as He is one with the Father (see John 17:11). Our being in unity with God and each other is what the greatest commandment will produce. The Lord our God is one and we are in Him.

> **John 17:11 NKJV**
> Now I am no longer in the world, but these are in the world, and I come to You. Holy Father, keep through Your name those whom You have given Me, that they may be one as We are.

In recent decades, the Lord has been restoring the fivefold ministries of the apostle, prophet, evangelist, pastor, and teacher. God is restoring His kingdom government in order to equip all of His people for the work of the ministry.

The work of this fivefold ministry is to continue until all of God's people come fully into the unity of faith and His people measure up to the fullness and stature of Jesus (see Ephesians 4:11-13).

> **Ephesians 4:11-13 NKJV**
>
> (11) And He Himself gave some to be apostles, some prophets, some evangelists, and some pastors and teachers,
>
> (12) for the equipping of the saints for the work of ministry, for the edifying of the body of Christ,
>
> (13) till we all come to the unity of the faith and of the knowledge of the Son of God, to a perfect man, to the measure of the stature of the fullness of Christ;

It's time for the church to come together in the unity of the faith. This will happen as more and more of God's people repent of unbelief and fully yield to His Holy Spirit.

THE POWER OF UNITY

Consider what Jesus said about unity in Matthew 18:18-20.

> **Matthew 18:18-20 NKJV**
> (18) "Assuredly, I say to you, whatever you bind on earth will be bound in heaven, and whatever you loose on earth will be loosed in heaven.
>
> (19) "Again I say to you that if two of you agree on earth concerning anything that they ask, it will be done for them by My Father in heaven.
>
> (20) For where two or three are gathered together in My name, I am there in the midst of them."

We see in Matthew 18:18-20 that when there are at least two or three people gathered in unity that amazing things happen. When they bind or loose it will be effective and powerful. Whatever they ask for will be done for them by our Father in Heaven. And according to verse 20, Jesus will be there in the midst of them!

6

THE POWER OF IMAGINATION

**Then I heard the Lord say,
"You can teach them
The Power of Imagination."**

THE POWER OF IMAGINATION

Your imagination was God's idea. Adam used his imagination to co-labor with his Father God during creation. God brought all the animals to Adam to see what he would call them. As I mentioned previously, whatever Adam "called" each animal became its "*name*."

The Hebrew word "*call*" means to "*declare*," similar to prophesying. The Hebrew word "*name*" means a mark of individuality. It reflects the essence of the person or thing named.

I believe Adam assigned characteristics, traits, and temperament of each species of animal.

When Adam sinned against God he became separated from his Father. The devil has been busy using man's imagination to create evil and disrupt creation since then.

> **Genesis 8:20-21 AMPC**
> (20) And Noah built an altar to the Lord and took of every clean [four-footed] animal and of every clean fowl or bird and offered burnt offerings on the altar.
>
> (21) When the Lord smelled the pleasing odor [a scent of satisfaction to His heart], the Lord said to Himself, I will never again curse the

> ground because of man, for the imagination (the strong desire) of man's heart is evil and wicked from his youth; neither will I ever again smite and destroy every living thing, as I have done.

Jesus described Himself as the one who is, who was, and is to come (see Revelation 1:4). We are created to reflect Him.

There are three connected aspects to each person that works in a way that affects their entire being. Each part directly affects the other two parts. The part that is, was, and is to come.

In other words, our soul is made of three parts. Our memories, our conscience, and our imaginations reflect this three-part aspect.

Memories are the part of us that was. Our conscience is the part that is. And our imagination is the part of us that is to come.

As we are continually sanctified by the Holy Spirit and God's word these three aspects become sanctified and more in tuned with the Lord. God can cleanse our memories as we, by faith, apply the shed blood of Jesus to reoccurring, unclean, or bad memories.

Our conscience is where God placed His laws in us. Our conscience is very sensitive to holiness when we first come of age. As time goes by and we sin against God our conscience can become less sensitive or even dull.

Once we are born again we can cleanse our conscience by faith with the blood of Jesus. This will restore a wonderful sensitivity to God's holy standards. This is a great thing because it will keep us synchronized and one with Jesus.

As our memories and our conscience becomes more sanctified, our imaginations also become more clean. As our imaginations become more clean it is more synchronized with the thoughts and purposes of Jesus.

As our imagination gets cleaner and more yielded to God they become expressions of His dreams. In other words, God's dreams become our dreams.

Philippians 2:13 NKJV
... for it is God who works in you both to will and to do for His good pleasure.

Our Father wants our imagination to be sanctified and clean because He wants us to be able to freely dream and create. As we express the ability to be creative we are to a greater degree reflecting our Father who is Creator.

THE POWER OF IMAGINATION

Once again let's visit Mark 12:29-30, where one of the religious leaders asked Jesus what the greatest commandment was.

> **Mark 12:29-30 NKJV**
> (29) Jesus answered him, "The first of all the commandments is: 'HEAR, O ISRAEL, THE LORD OUR GOD, THE LORD IS ONE.
>
> (30) AND YOU SHALL LOVE THE LORD YOUR GOD WITH ALL YOUR HEART, WITH ALL YOUR SOUL, WITH ALL YOUR MIND, AND WITH ALL YOUR STRENGTH.' This is the first commandment.

Notice the word "MIND" in Mark 12:30. The original word for "*mind*" is dianoia which means the mental faculty and it's exercise of the imagination, mind, and understanding.

God wants us to love Him with all our heart, soul, minds, and strength. We are to love Him with every aspect of our natural and spiritual being.

We are to love the Lord our God with our deep thoughts and imaginations. We are to love and worship Him with our daydreams and what we fantasize about.

The prophet Joel prophesied about the coming

THE POWER OF IMAGINATION

day of Pentecost when God would pour out His Holy Spirit. One of the things He said was, "Your old men shall dream dreams" (see Joel 2:28).

> **Joel 2:28 WEB**
> It will happen afterward, that I will pour out my Spirit on all flesh; and your sons and your daughters will prophesy. Your old men will dream dreams. Your young men will see visions.

The first word in Joel 2:28 for "*dream*" is a verb. This word is used to mean fantasizing things in the book of Jude (see Jude 1:8). To dream is an action taken by the person. The word "*dream*" in that context is something a person does by a conscious willful act similar to daydreaming or fantasizing.

The second word used for "*dream*" in Joel 2:28 is a noun. This speaks of something that is produced from the previous action taken or from the dreaming. Dreaming or fantasizing produces dreams.

When the prophet used the term "*old men*" in Joel 2:28, I believe this represented the spiritual maturity of a person. A 10-year-old child could be an old man in the Spirit. These spiritually mature saints will use their imagination to co-labor with God as Adam did in naming the animals during the creation events (see Genesis 2:19).

> **Ephesians 3:20-21 AMPC**
> (20) Now to Him Who, by (in consequence of) the [action of His] power that is at work within us, is able to [carry out His purpose and] do superabundantly, far over and above all that we [dare] ask or think [infinitely beyond our highest prayers, desires, thoughts, hopes, or dreams]--
>
> (21) To Him be glory in the church and in Christ Jesus throughout all generations forever and ever. Amen (so be it).

Jesus taught that sin committed in the heart is considered to be real from a spiritual vantage point. It isn't enough for someone to not physically commit adultery because if the person commits adultery in their heart then it is considered to have been done (see Matthew 5:27-28).

Accordingly, what is done in our heart is literally considered to be real from Heaven's vantage point.

What occurs in our heart is so real that judgment will be based on it. If sinful things that occur in the heart are real in the spirit then holy things are also considered to be real.

THE POWER OF IMAGINATION

Matthew 5:27-28 AMPC

(27) You have heard that it was said, You shall not commit adultery.

(28) But I say to you that everyone who so much as looks at a woman with evil desire for her has already committed adultery with her in his heart.

Matthew 15:18-20 AMPC

(18) But whatever comes out of the mouth comes from the heart, and this is what makes a man unclean and defiles [him].

(19) For out of the heart come evil thoughts (reasonings and disputings and designs) such as murder, adultery, sexual vice, theft, false witnessing, slander, and irreverent speech.

(20) These are what make a man unclean and defile [him]; but eating with unwashed hands does not make him unclean or defile [him].

Matthew 12:34-35 AMPC

(34) You offspring of vipers! How can you speak good things when you are evil (wicked)? For out of the fullness (the overflow, the superabundance) of the heart the mouth speaks.

THE POWER OF IMAGINATION

(35) The good man from his inner good treasure flings forth good things, and the evil man out of his inner evil storehouse flings forth evil things.

2 Timothy 2:22 AMPC
Shun youthful lusts and flee from them, and aim at and pursue righteousness (all that is virtuous and good, right living, conformity to the will of God in thought, word, and deed); [and aim at and pursue] faith, love, [and] peace (harmony and concord with others) in fellowship with all [Christians], who call upon the Lord out of a pure heart.

There is a verse in the book of Job that indicates how important it is to have our thoughts and imaginations in line with God.

Job had been greatly afflicted by the devil after God lifted His hedge of protection from around him. Job then lost everything. He then said something that provides a key revelation. Job said, "For the thing I greatly feared has come upon me, And what I dreaded has happened to me" (see Job 3:25).

Apparently Job had spent much time thinking about all the things that could go wrong in his life. He lived within God's fence of protection but in fear.

God later fully restored everything to Job. In fact,

God gave Job more than he originally had. Each of the things Job had lost and later had restored were specifically mentioned.

However, there is no mention of God putting the hedge of protection back around Job. Apparently Job had an encounter with God that delivered him from the fear that had previously occupied his thoughts.

Job had an encounter with God that caused an awakening within about God. In a manner of speaking, he had a face to face encounter with God. This new revelation released a reverent fear of God.

The fear of God caused all other fears to vanish and consequently elevated Job to a higher position of authority over the devil.

> **Job 42:5 NKJV**
> "I have heard of You by the hearing of the ear,
> But now my eye sees You."

If bad desires or dreams within our hearts are considered to be real then it holds true that good dreams within our hearts are also just as real in the spirit realm.

What occurs in someone's heart is more real than what occurs in the natural realm. What occurs in people's hearts is considered to be so real that judgment will be applied according to what occurs there. This is because everything in the natural world originated from the spiritual realm (see Hebrews 11:3). What exists in the spirit realm is more real and permanent than the natural world.

Our imagination abides in the spiritual realm because they are connected to our spirits. What occurs in this area of our being will manifest into our natural lives.

The Lord recently showed me that daydreaming or fantasizing about something that brought Him honor was considered as prophecy from His point of view. So when we use our imagination to dream things that glorify the Lord we are loving Him with all our minds including our imagination.

He will use our sanctified imagination to bring forth things in a similar way that things are brought forth through a prophetic proclamation.

Remember what occurs in our hearts and minds is considered more real than the things we can observe in the natural world. A sanctified imagination is in unity and yielded to the Lord.

Psalms 145:19 NKJV
He will fulfill the desire of those who

fear Him; He also will hear their cry and save them.

Proverbs 10:24 AMPC
The fear of the wicked will come upon him, And the desire of the righteous will be granted.

John 15:7 NKJV
If you abide in Me, and My words abide in you, you will ask what you desire, and it shall be done for you.

Another aspect of our imagination that was shown to me was that our imagination can become a bridge that connects victories from the past to victories in the future. These prophetic victories are then brought into the now as God honors the desires of our sanctified imaginations.

Take a look at the account of little David and the giant Goliath (see 1 Samuel 17: 1-53).

The Philistine army had come up against the army of Israel. The giant Goliath came out and mocked the Army of Israel. He demanded that they send forward a champion that he could fight. Whichever side lost would become the slaves of the other side. All of the Israeli soldiers were terrified and fled at the sight of the giant.

THE POWER OF IMAGINATION

David, a teenager at the time, was sent by his father to deliver food to his older brothers that were with the Israeli army. When David arrived at the battlefield he could see that Goliath the giant was mocking the Israeli army and their God.

David then asked the soldiers what would be done for the man who defeated the giant. They told him that the man who defeated the giant would get to marry the king's daughter and would not have to pay future taxes.

Then David's older brother overheard his conversation with the soldiers and became angry at him. He accused David of being prideful and insolent. David then said, "What have I done now? Is there not a cause?"

David was jealous for the name of God and His people. David's challenge to the soldiers was reported to King Saul. David then told Saul that he should take courage because he would kill the giant. Saul responded that he would not be able to win because he was only a young untrained man.

But David began to rehearse past victories. David then told the king of his experience as a shepherd when a bear and later a lion came to take one of his

THE POWER OF IMAGINATION

sheep. David told the king that he had rescued the sheep out of the mouth of the bear and later the lion. He then said as he killed a lion and a bear he would deal with Goliath the same way.

> **1 Samuel 17:37 NKJV**
> Moreover David said, "The LORD, who delivered me from the paw of the lion and from the paw of the bear, He will deliver me from the hand of this Philistine." And Saul said to David, "Go, and the LORD be with you!"

David remembered the times that the Lord helped him with the lion and the bear. And then imagined and declared that God would do the same against Goliath. David took testimonies of God's deliverance from the past and by faith imagined the same into the future.

Goliath mocked David, the Israeli army, and their God. But David made bold proclamations of what he was about to do to Goliath, pay attention to verse 46 in the following verses.

> **1 Samuel 17:42-46 NKJV**
> (42) And when the Philistine looked about and saw David, he disdained him; for he was

only a youth, ruddy and good-looking.

(43) So the Philistine said to David, "Am I a dog, that you come to me with sticks?" And the Philistine cursed David by his gods.

(44) And the Philistine said to David, "Come to me, and I will give your flesh to the birds of the air and the beasts of the field!"

(45) Then David said to the Philistine, "You come to me with a sword, with a spear, and with a javelin. But I come to you in the name of the LORD of hosts, the God of the armies of Israel, whom you have defied.

(46) This day the LORD will deliver you into my hand, and I will strike you and take your head from you. And this day I will give the carcasses of the camp of the Philistines to the birds of the air and the wild beasts of the earth, that all the earth may know that there is a God in Israel.

All that David imagined and declared out loud were supernaturally fulfilled by the hand of the Lord. Victories from David's past relationship with the Lord were prophesied into the future through his imagination.

THE POWER OF IMAGINATION

Goliath also proclaimed what he would do to David but it was David's desire that was fulfilled against Goliath.

Proverbs 16:3 AMPC
Roll your works upon the Lord [commit and trust them wholly to Him; He will cause your thoughts to become agreeable to His will, and] so shall your plans be established and succeed.

Proverbs 10:24 NKJV
The thing a wicked man fears shall come upon him, but the desire of the [uncompromisingly] righteous shall be granted.

Psalms 10:3-4 NKJV
(3) For the wicked boasts of his heart's desire; He blesses the greedy and renounces the LORD.

(4) The wicked in his proud countenance does not seek God; God is in none of his thoughts.

Ezekiel 36:26-27 NKJV
(26) I will give you a new heart and put a new spirit within you; I will take the heart of stone

out of your flesh and give you a heart of flesh.

(27) I will put My Spirit within you and cause you to walk in My statutes, and you will keep My judgments and do them.

Proverbs 12:5 NKJV
The thoughts of the righteous are right, But the counsels of the wicked are deceitful.

Isaiah 55:6-9 NKJV
(6) Seek the LORD while He may be found, Call upon Him while He is near.

(7) Let the wicked forsake his way, And the unrighteous man his thoughts; Let him return to the LORD, And He will have mercy on him; And to our God, For He will abundantly pardon.

(8) "For My thoughts are not your thoughts, Nor are your ways My ways," says the LORD.

(9) "For as the heavens are higher than the earth, So are My ways higher than your ways, And My thoughts than your thoughts.

Consider the verses found in Revelation 12:9-11 about the battle between God's kingdom and the devil. They contain keys to overcoming the devil with our imagination. Verse 11 says, "And they overcame him by the blood of the Lamb and by the word of their testimony, and they did not love their lives to the death."

They overcame by the following:
The blood of Jesus.
The word of their testimony.
They loved the life of Jesus more than their own.

The blood of Jesus cancels all accusations and ordinances against us. With His own blood Jesus… "disarmed principalities and powers, He made a public spectacle of them, triumphing over them in it" (see Colossians 2:15).

The saints overcome the devil by trading their lives for the life of Jesus (see Colossians 1:27). They accepted His offer of entering into His rest. They lived through Jesus.

And they overcame by the word of their testimony. The original Greek word "*testimony*" is interesting. It means to testify like a witness of past events. But it is also used to mean what one testifies concerning future events—like that of a prophet. See the following definition of the original Greek word for "*testimony*."

THE POWER OF IMAGINATION

Thayer Definition: "Testimony"- marturia
"1) a testifying
1a) the office committed to the prophets of testifying concerning future events
2) what one testifies, testimony, i.e. before a judge."

Revelations 12:9-11 NKJV
(9) So the great dragon was cast out, that serpent of old, called the Devil and Satan, who deceives the whole world; he was cast to the earth, and his angels were cast out with him.

(10) Then I heard a loud voice saying in heaven, "Now salvation, and strength, and the kingdom of our God, and the power of His Christ have come, for the accuser of our brethren, who accused them before our God day and night, has been cast down.

(11) And they overcame him by the blood of the Lamb and by the word of their testimony, and they did not love their lives to the death.

We see another encounter in Revelation 19:10 that gives more insight to overcoming the enemy.

During a profound encounter while in Heaven, the Apostle John found himself before a heavenly person and then fell at his feet. I believe this heavenly person was a saint. The saint then said, "See that you do not do that! I am your fellow servant, and of your brethren who have the testimony of Jesus. Worship God! For the testimony of Jesus is the spirit of prophecy."

He said he had "the testimony of Jesus." That word "testimony" is the same Greek word used for "testimony" in Revelation 12:11.

Later in the verse the saint said, "For the testimony of Jesus is the spirit of prophecy." Take a look at the definition for the original Greek word for "prophecy."

Thayer Definition: "Prophecy" - prophēteia

"1) prophecy

1a) a discourse emanating from divine inspiration and declaring the purposes of God, whether by reproving and admonishing the wicked, or comforting the afflicted, or revealing things hidden; especially by foretelling future events.

We see from these verses in Revelation 12:11 and 19:10 that our testimonies are past victories won by our Lord. The testimony of Jesus is the spirit of prophecy or the essence by which we can declare future victories through our sanctified imagination. Our imaginations can become bridges that connect past victories into the future. These become greater victories which are prophesied into the present by speaking in faith.

These victorious imaginations will be received as worship by our Lord.

> **Revelation 19:10 NKJV**
> And I fell at his feet to worship him. But he said to me, "See that you do not do that! I am your fellow servant, and of your brethren who have the testimony of Jesus. Worship God! For the testimony of Jesus is the spirit of prophecy."

7
HE WILL GIVE US REST

The Lord then said to me,
"I will give them rest soon. They will cease from their own work and move into Mine.

We are going to start taking over.

Born to Rule. That's you all."

The Lord has been talking to me about rest for several years. There is an incident that happened in 2014 when He used an encounter to confirm what He had been saying.

I felt the Lord directing me to research raw milk. This connected with me about the rest of the Lord. In the Bible God referred to the Promised Land as the land of rest and a land flowing with milk and honey (see Deuteronomy 12:10).

It seemed prophetic, so I researched and found a small family owned dairy that sold raw milk. My daughter and I drove there and bought some milk. We were excited as we approached the desolate main highway to go back home.

Then as we were merging onto the highway we were passed by a very unique vehicle. It looked like an extended white six door limousine. Some of the windows were rolled down. It had longhorn horns mounted on the front that spanned at least 6 feet. Two large American flags were mounted on each rear fender.

There were two young athletic looking men with shoulder length hair riding inside. They casually looked over at us as they slowly passed by. Then we saw something amazing. There was a sign on the side of the car that read "Got Milk?" We were stunned and excited at the same time. A few moments later we gathered our thoughts. We decided to look back for them but they were nowhere to be found.

I believe these were heavenly messengers sent to give confirmation from our Lord.

Jesus desires to give us rest. He wants us to be yoked or connected to Him so He can carry us. He wants to release His power and life through us. The works He intends to do through us have been established since before the foundation of the world (see Hebrews 4:3).

> **Matthew 11:28-30 NKJV**
> (28) Come to Me, all you who labor and are heavy laden, and I will give you rest.
>
> (29) Take My yoke upon you and learn from Me, for I am gentle and lowly in heart, and you will find rest for your souls.
>
> (30) For My yoke is easy and My burden is light."

What does it mean to enter into His rest? Paul exhorts us to enter the rest of the Lord in Hebrews chapters 3 and 4. He used the account of the children of Israel after God delivered them from Egypt and brought them into the desert.

God said, through Moses, that He was going to bring them into the Promised Land and they would possess it. God described the place as the land of rest (see Deuteronomy 12:10). It was a place flowing with milk and honey. It was a place brimming with abundance and prosperity!

There were also mighty adversaries in the land. And these vile people would have to be conquered and removed from the land. Once the children of Israel came to the edge of the land of rest along the Jordan River, they were instructed to send twelve spies to spy out the land.

The twelve spies returned with samples of the amazing fruit and produce from the land. However, ten of the twelve men gave a bad report to the people as they said there were giants in the land and there was no way Israel could defeat them. These ten spies caused all the people to fear and complain.

Only Joshua and Caleb gave a good report. They tried to exhort the people to believe God's promise that He would deliver the land into their hands.

The people heard God's word but it wasn't mixed with faith. Their unbelief and rebellion angered God.

HE WILL GIVE US REST

So He declared that they would not enter into the land of rest. And only Joshua and Caleb would be allowed to enter in along with the next generation. The rebellious generation however would all perish in the desert over the course of forty years.

> **Hebrews 4:1-3 NKJV**
> (1) Therefore, since a promise remains of entering His rest, let us fear lest any of you seem to have come short of it.
>
> (2) For indeed the gospel was preached to us as well as to them; but the word which they heard did not profit them, not being mixed with faith in those who heard it.
>
> (3) For we who have believed do enter that rest, as He has said: "SO I SWORE IN MY WRATH, 'THEY SHALL NOT ENTER MY REST,' although the works were finished from the foundation of the world.

Entering into God's rest is not something we do after we die and go to heaven. According to Hebrews 4:3, entering His rest is something we do while believing in Jesus.

Paul explains what the "rest" of God represents in Hebrews 4:10. To enter into God's rest means that we have ceased from our own works. We are to cease from our own works just as God ceased from His on the seventh day of creation. And He ceased from His works because it was complete.

Hebrews 4:9-11 NKJV
(9) There remains therefore a rest for the people of God.

(10) For he who has entered His rest has himself also ceased from his works as God did from His.

(11) Let us therefore be diligent to enter that rest, lest anyone fall according to the same example of disobedience.

God commanded Israel to honor the Sabbath day in order to honor Him as Creator. This pointed to God's plan for restoring all things through His people as they lived by faith (see Matthew 17:11). By faith, we cease from our own works which will manifest His life and works in and through us. This is the rest of God.

John 6:28-29 NKJV
(28) Then they said to Him, "What shall we do, that we may work the works of God?"

(29) Jesus answered and said to them, "This is the work of God, that you believe in Him whom He sent."

There is a prophecy in Isaiah chapter 30 that can give insight regarding the need for faith and rest. The prophecy described in verses 1 through 17 contains comments by God regarding the predicament that Judah found themselves in.

Assyria was attacking the northern kingdom and now the fierce enemy was coming for Judah. Judah panicked and went to Egypt instead of God for help. God expressed His displeasure in Isaiah 30:1-3.

> **Isaiah 30:1-3 NKJV**
>
> (1) "Woe to the rebellious children," says the LORD, "Who take counsel, but not of Me, And who devise plans, but not of My Spirit, That they may add sin to sin;
>
> (2) Who walk to go down to Egypt, And have not asked My advice, To strengthen themselves in the strength of Pharaoh, And to trust in the shadow of Egypt!
>
> (3) Therefore the strength of Pharaoh Shall be your shame, And trust in the shadow of Egypt Shall be your humiliation.

God's people plotted various ways of escape, but God said that none of their own plans would work. Then God provided the way out of their great calamity.

HE WILL GIVE US REST

God said, "In returning and rest you shall be saved; In quietness and confidence shall be your strength" (see Isaiah 30:15).

God said they needed to return, in other words repent. And they needed to "rest" or look to His works. He then said they needed quietness and confidence—or faith. They would enter into His rest and this would mean ceasing from their own resources and allowing God to manifest His on their behalf. Sadly they refused God.

> **Isaiah 30:15-16 NKJV**
> (15) For thus says the Lord GOD, the Holy One of Israel: "In returning and rest you shall be saved; In quietness and confidence shall be your strength." But you would not,
>
> (16) And you said, "No, for we will flee on horses"—Therefore you shall flee! And, "We will ride on swift horses"—Therefore those who pursue you shall be swift!

Moses knew there was a better way and longed for it. He expressed his desire in the following verses.

> **Psalms 90:16-17 AMPC**
> (16) Let Your work [the signs of Your power] be revealed to Your servants, and Your

[glorious] majesty to their children.

(17) And let the beauty and delightfulness and favor of the Lord our God be upon us; confirm and establish the work of our hands--yes, the work of our hands, confirm and establish it.

We must return to Jesus and repent of all unbelief. We must believe in Him. We must repent of making plans apart from His Spirit. Then we will cease from our own works. He will establish the work of our hands through us. His work will appear to us along with His glory. The beauty of the Lord will be upon us!

8

ZION IS COMING

I heard the Lord say,
"Zion is being established on the earth in various places.

Pockets of grace authority. Gathering of the remnant for healing the nations. Embassies of the Kingdom on the earth.

Let them rule and reign in righteousness."

ZION IS COMING

The Lord directed my family and I to move from the West Texas area to the Dallas area in November of 2019.

Shortly after moving we were going into the local supermarket and noticed a young man limping ahead of us. He was wearing athletic sweats and listening to headphones. I knew the Lord wanted us to pray for him so I caught up to him and asked if we could pray for him. I said, "I believe the Lord Jesus is going to heal you."

He said that his name was Zion and that he had severely twisted his ankle while playing on the basketball team. We asked Jesus to heal him and within seconds his ankle was totally healed!

Zion squealed and shouted with excitement as though he had just one the lottery. He started running around and shouting to everyone that his ankle was healed. I knew that this was a prophetic encounter.

In the nation of Israel people were considered to be very blessed just to be dwelling in the land. People who lived in Jerusalem were considered to be even more blessed. And those who lived in Zion were considered to be blessed most of all. Zion was the original City of David from which Jerusalem grew around.

ZION IS COMING

According to scripture, Zion is the place of God's throne and power (see Psalms 110:2). It was also the original city captured by King David and which became known as the City of David.

God has made amazing prophetic proclamations regarding Zion. Here are just a few:

> **Psalms 102:12-18 NKJV**
> (12) But You, O LORD, shall endure forever, And the remembrance of Your name to all generations.
>
> (13) You will arise and have mercy on Zion; For the time to favor her, Yes, the set time, has come.
>
> (14) For Your servants take pleasure in her stones, And show favor to her dust.
>
> (15) So the nations shall fear the name of the LORD, And all the kings of the earth Your glory.
>
> (16) For the LORD shall build up Zion; He shall appear in His glory.
>
> (17) He shall regard the prayer of the destitute, And shall not despise their prayer.
>
> (18) This will be written for the generation to come, That a people yet to be created may

ZION IS COMING

praise the LORD.

The time has come for God's favor to Zion. v13.
He shall appear in His Glory. v16.
This is written for a generation to come. v18.

Psalms 2:6 NKJV
"Yet I have set My King On My holy hill of Zion."

His King sits in Zion.

Psalms 9:11 NKJV
Sing praises to the LORD, who dwells in Zion! Declare His deeds among the people.

The Lord dwells in Zion.

Psalms 50:2 NKJV
Out of Zion, the perfection of beauty, God will shine forth.

God will shine forth out of Zion.

Psalms 87:5-6 NKJV
(5) And of Zion it will be said, "This one and that one were born in her; And the Most High Himself shall establish her."

(6) The LORD will record, When He registers the peoples: "This one was born there." Selah.

God Himself will register and establish those born there.

ZION IS COMING

Psalms 110:2 NKJV
The LORD shall send the rod of Your strength out of Zion. Rule in the midst of Your enemies!

The rod of God's strength comes out of Zion.

Psalms 132:13-17 NKJV
(13) For the LORD has chosen Zion; He has desired it for His dwelling place:

(14) "This is My resting place forever; Here I will dwell, for I have desired it.

(15) I will abundantly bless her provision; I will satisfy her poor with bread.

(16) I will also clothe her priests with salvation, And her saints shall shout aloud for joy.

(17) There I will make the horn of David grow; I will prepare a lamp for My Anointed.

> *God has chosen Zion for His dwelling place.*
> *Zion is His resting place forever.*
> *He will abundantly bless her provision.*
> *He will satisfy with bread.*
> *He will clothe her priests with salvation.*
> *The horn of David will grow.*
> *There will be a lamp for His anointed.*

These verses regarding Zion were prophetically

pointing toward the coming King Jesus and His Kingdom. We can glean eternal truths and revelation from them.

Paul indicated in Hebrews chapter 8 that the things and ordinances recorded in the Old Testament were copies and shadows of the real heavenly things. The tabernacle and Ark of the Covenant were pointing the way to access the coming King and His Kingdom.

> **Hebrews 8:1-6 AMPC**
> (1) NOW THE main point of what we have to say is this: We have such a High Priest, One Who is seated at the right hand of the majestic [God] in heaven,
>
> (2) As officiating Priest, a Minister in the holy places and in the true tabernacle which is erected not by man but by the Lord.
>
> (3) For every high priest is appointed to offer up gifts and sacrifices; so it is essential for this [High Priest] to have some offering to make also.
>
> (4) If then He were still living on earth, He would not be a priest at all, for there are [already priests] who offer the gifts in accordance with the Law.

(5) [But these offer] service [merely] as a pattern and as a foreshadowing of [what has its true existence and reality in] the heavenly sanctuary. For when Moses was about to erect the tabernacle, he was warned by God, saying, See to it that you make it all [exactly] according to the copy (the model) which was shown to you on the mountain.

(6) But as it now is, He [Christ] has acquired a [priestly] ministry which is as much superior and more excellent [than the old] as the covenant (the agreement) of which He is the Mediator (the Arbiter, Agent) is superior and more excellent, [because] it is enacted and rests upon more important (sublimer, higher, and nobler) promises.

In Hebrews chapter 11 Paul presents some of the past champions of faith and the many exploits accomplished through their lives.

Then in chapter 12 Paul directs our gaze upward and forward. He states that we are currently surrounded by so great a cloud of witnesses and should lay aside things that slow us down. He goes on to say that we should look unto Jesus, the author and finisher of our faith.

Paul wants us to gaze upward to Jesus and be

strengthened by the reality of His Divine Presence (see Colossians 3:1). Jesus is the initiator and the finisher of our faith so we must look to Him!

> **Hebrews 12:1-2 NKJV**
> (1) Therefore we also, since we are surrounded by so great a cloud of witnesses, let us lay aside every weight, and the sin which so easily ensnares us, and let us run with endurance the race that is set before us,
>
> (2) looking unto Jesus, the author and finisher of our faith, who for the joy that was set before Him endured the cross, despising the shame, and has sat down at the right hand of the throne of God.

Notice that Paul said "we are" surrounded by a cloud of witnesses and then he says that we should look at Jesus. The Holy Spirit moving through Paul was trying to help us see the reality of the heavenly Zion.

Paul then used the prophetic revelation and understanding of Zion and how it relates to Jesus and His Kingdom. Slowly read the following verses in Hebrews 12:18-26 about what Zion means for us today.

ZION IS COMING

Hebrews 12:18-26 NKJV
(18) For you have not come to the mountain that may be touched and that burned with fire, and to blackness and darkness and tempest,

(19) and the sound of a trumpet and the voice of words, so that those who heard it begged that the word should not be spoken to them anymore.

(20) (For they could not endure what was commanded: "AND IF SO MUCH AS A BEAST TOUCHES THE MOUNTAIN, IT SHALL BE STONED OR SHOT WITH AN ARROW."

(21) And so terrifying was the sight that Moses said, "I AM EXCEEDINGLY AFRAID AND TREMBLING.")

(22) But you have come to Mount Zion and to the city of the living God, the heavenly Jerusalem, to an innumerable company of angels,

(23) to the general assembly and church of the firstborn who are registered in heaven, to God the Judge of all, to the spirits of just men made perfect,

(24) to Jesus the Mediator of the new covenant, and to the blood of sprinkling that speaks better things than that of Abel.

(25) See that you do not refuse Him who speaks. For if they did not escape who refused Him who spoke on earth, much more shall we not escape if we turn away from Him who speaks from heaven,

(26) whose voice then shook the earth; but now He has promised, saying, "YET ONCE MORE I SHAKE NOT ONLY THE EARTH, BUT ALSO HEAVEN."

I heard the Lord say that Zion is coming. These verses can give us some understanding of what this means to us today.

Paul starts out remembering how the children of Israel refused God at Mount Sinai because of the terror they saw and heard. It was so shocking that even Moses was terrified.

Then Paul contrasts what the children of Israel were offered to what we are being offered today. He clearly states that we HAVE come to Mount Zion (see Hebrews 12:22)! Not will come but HAVE come to the City of the Living God, the heavenly Jerusalem!

Take a look at what is included in this place we come to by faith:

- **Innumerable company of angels, v22.**
- **The general assembly, v23.**

- **Church of the firstborn registered in heaven, v23.**
- **God the Judge of all, v23.**
- **The spirits of just men made perfect, v23.**
- **Jesus the Mediator of the new covenant, v23.**
- **The blood of sprinkling that speaks better things than that of Abel, v24.**

These are all seen and found in Heaven. Paul states that we HAVE come to this mount Zion or heavenly Jerusalem. This is NOW going to become reality in many places.

Remember what Jesus said while teaching His disciples to pray:

> **Matthew 6:10 AMPC**
> Your kingdom come, Your will be done on earth as it is in heaven.

The account of Jesus being transfigured gives clear insight regarding God's kingdom coming and His will being done on earth as it is in heaven (see Matthew 16:28).

> **Matthew 17:1-6 NKJV**
> (1) Now after six days Jesus took Peter, James, and John his brother, led them up on a high mountain by themselves;

(2) and He was transfigured before them. His face shone like the sun, and His clothes became as white as the light.

(3) And behold, Moses and Elijah appeared to them, talking with Him.

(4) Then Peter answered and said to Jesus, "Lord, it is good for us to be here; if You wish, let us make here three tabernacles: one for You, one for Moses, and one for Elijah."

(5) While he was still speaking, behold, a bright cloud overshadowed them; and suddenly a voice came out of the cloud, saying, "This is My beloved Son, in whom I am well pleased. Hear Him!"

(6) And when the disciples heard it, they fell on their faces and were greatly afraid.

Jesus took Peter, James, and John up to the top of a mountain. Suddenly Jesus' appearance dramatically changed. His face shone like the sun. His clothes were luminous white. And there were two deceased saints standing there talking to Jesus!

This was a meeting of the heavenly congregation and the church on earth. Elijah and Moses were there talking to Jesus. Elijah represented the power of the Spirit and Moses represented the law. And Jesus is the fulfillment of the law and the power of the Spirit.

Peter got nervous and started talking. He suggested they build tabernacles or little huts for Jesus, Elijah, and Moses. Then a bright cloud overshadowed them and the Father joined in on the meeting telling Peter to listen to Jesus.

Peter was only doing what good Jewish guys did during the Feast of Tabernacles. They traditionally would build small huts out of branches to commemorate when Israel lived in the wilderness and under the cloud of God's Presence.

Peter had recently received a revelation from the Father that Jesus was the Messiah (see Matthew 16:16-17). Perhaps Peter had just received another revelation about what the Feast of Tabernacles pointed to.

In any event, Peter beheld the transfiguration of Jesus and immediately thought of building tabernacles.

The Feast of Tabernacles is the third of three main Feasts that Jewish males were to observe in Jerusalem each year. The first two feasts are Passover and Feast of Weeks. These pointed to the Crucifixion of Jesus and the Day of Pentecost.

What is the Feast of Tabernacles? The Feast of

Tabernacles marked the time when God made Israel live in booths or huts while in the wilderness. It was also a time when He overshadowed His people with His Presence, or Spirit (see Leviticus 23:42-43). The Feast of Tabernacles was also a time to officially remember the law He had given them (see Deuteronomy 31:10-11).

The Feast of Tabernacles memorialized the Presence of God and the law of God. Moses, representing the law, and Elijah, representing the Spirit, were present with Jesus under the canopy of God during the transfiguration of Jesus.

No wonder Peter wanted to build tabernacles for Jesus, Moses, and Elijah during the transfiguration of Jesus. Peter connected what was happening there to the Feast of Tabernacles. But now the real thing had returned. God was tabernacling among men!

> **Exodus 40:34-38 AMPC**
> (34) Then the cloud [the Shekinah, God's visible presence] covered the Tent of Meeting, and the glory of the Lord filled the tabernacle!
>
> (35) And Moses was not able to enter the Tent of Meeting because the cloud remained upon it, and the glory of the Lord filled the tabernacle.

(36) In all their journeys, whenever the cloud was taken up from over the tabernacle, the Israelites went onward;

(37) But if the cloud was not taken up, they did not journey on till the day that it was taken up.

(38) For throughout all their journeys the cloud of the Lord was upon the tabernacle by day, and fire was in it by night, in the sight of all the house of Israel.

John 1:14 AMPC
And the Word (Christ) became flesh (human, incarnate) and tabernacled (fixed His tent of flesh, lived awhile) among us; and we [actually] saw His glory (His honor, His majesty), such glory as an only begotten son receives from his father, full of grace (favor, loving-kindness) and truth.

Jesus was the Word, or law, that had become a man in the power of the Spirit. The Father overshadowed Jesus at the very beginning of His walk as "Son of Man." The Powerful Person of the Holy Spirit overshadowed Mary as the Son of God was being conceived as Son of Man.

ZION IS COMING

Luke 1:35 AMPC
(35) Then the angel said to her, The Holy Spirit will come upon you, and the power of the Most High will overshadow you [like a shining cloud]; and so the holy (pure, sinless) Thing (Offspring) which shall be born of you will be called the Son of God.

Let's look at the word "overshadow" in that verse describing how Jesus would be conceived.

> *Overshadow - Strong's Hebrew and Greek Dictionaries - to cast a shade upon, that is, (by analogy) to envelop in a haze of brilliancy; figuratively to invest with preternatural influence.*

God's will was being done on earth as it was in heaven. Heaven had come down to earth. The church in Heaven had intersected with the church on earth.

Moses' face radiated like the sun after being in the Father's Presence previously on Mount Sinai. He had to cover his face because the people couldn't even look at him due to the brightness. The glory was fading on Moses because of what was to come.

Why didn't Jesus come down the mountain shining with God's glory as well? He still had to go to the cross. It was necessary that He go to the cross as a lamb. However, He is now returning as a lion.

Jesus wasn't born into the world for His own benefit but ours. He wasn't crucified and raised from the dead for His own benefit. And He wasn't transfigured for His gain but for ours.

Everything Jesus did was to restore what was lost by Adam in the garden of Eden (see Matthew 17:11). This includes what occurred during His transfiguration.

Jesus appeared to His disciples after the resurrection and gave them their assignment.

> **John 20:21-22 AMPC**
> (21) Then Jesus said to them again, Peace to you! [Just] as the Father has sent Me forth, so I am sending you.
>
> (22) And having said this, He breathed on them and said to them, Receive the Holy Spirit!

We must be willing to believe Jesus NOW. Jesus said that we would do what He did and what He does.

> **John 14:12 AMPC**
> I assure you, most solemnly I tell you, if anyone steadfastly believes in Me, he will himself be

able to do the things that I do; and he will do even greater things than these, because I go to the Father.

1 John 4:17 AMPC
In this [union and communion with Him] love is brought to completion and attains perfection with us, that we may have confidence for the day of judgment [with assurance and boldness to face Him], because as He is, so are we in this world.

He didn't place any precondition to this promise except "believe." He didn't place any time condition or limitation to this promise of doing what He did.

God is reconciling all things to Himself through Jesus. Because of this there is a reconciliation occurring between heaven and earth.

Colossians 1:19-20 NKJV
(19) For it pleased the Father that in Him all the fullness should dwell,

(20) and by Him to reconcile all things to Himself, by Him, whether things on earth or things in heaven, having made peace through the blood of His cross.

> **Ephesians 1:10 NKJV**
> that in the dispensation of the fullness of the times He might gather together in one all things in Christ, both which are in heaven and which are on earth—in Him.

Nicodemus, a religious leader, came to Jesus at night to say, "Rabbi, we know that You are a teacher come from God; for no one can do these signs that You do unless God is with him." Jesus then tells him that he must be born again. This confused the bible scholar so he asked how this could be.

> **John 3:4-5 NKJV**
> (4) Nicodemus said to Him, "How can a man be born when he is old? Can he enter a second time into his mother's womb and be born?"
>
> (5) Jesus answered, "Most assuredly, I say to you, unless one is born of water and the Spirit, he cannot enter the kingdom of God.

Slowly consider the following verses and the statements that Jesus made to Nicodemus after telling him that he must be born again.

> **John 3:12-13 NKJV**
> (12) If I have told you earthly things and you

do not believe, how will you believe if I tell you heavenly things?

(13) No one has ascended to heaven but He who came down from heaven, that is, the Son of Man who is in heaven.

Jesus said that being born again or entering the kingdom was earthly things in verse 12. That's right, entering the kingdom is an earthly thing according to Jesus.

The Lord goes on to say that He was the only one to descend from heaven and then to ascend. And in verse 13 He said that He was "in heaven" while there having that conversation with Nicodemus.

Notice these tremendous promises made by our Lord Jesus:

John 14:21-23 NKJV
(21) He who has My commandments and keeps them, it is he who loves Me. And he who loves Me will be loved by My Father, and I will love him and manifest Myself to him."

(22) Judas (not Iscariot) said to Him, "Lord, how is it that You will manifest Yourself to us, and not to the world?"

(23) Jesus answered and said to him, "If anyone

loves Me, he will keep My word; and My Father will love him, and We will come to him and make Our home with him.

Jesus said He will manifest Himself to us when we keep His commandments.

Notice the word "keeps" in verse 21 (see John 14:21-23 NKJV). In essence it means that we don't loose what He has said. We guard His word from being stolen by the devil (see Mark 4:14). It also means to behold, consider, or look upon.

Now let's look at the word "*manifest*" in verse 21 (see John 14:21-23 NKJV). It means "*to exhibit,*" "*to view,*" or "*appear.*" Consider the encounter Jesus had with His Father on the mount of transfiguration.

Jesus appeared to hundreds of His followers after being crucified and resurrected.

> **Matthew 28:5-9 AMPC**
> (5) But the angel said to the women, Do not be alarmed and frightened, for I know that you are looking for Jesus, Who was crucified.
>
> (6) He is not here; He has risen, as He said [He would do]. Come, see the place where He lay.
>
> (7) Then go quickly and tell His disciples, He has risen from the dead, and behold, He is

going before you to Galilee; there you will see Him. Behold, I have told you.

(8) So they left the tomb hastily with fear and great joy and ran to tell the disciples.

(9) And as they went, behold, Jesus met them and said, Hail (greetings)! And they went up to Him and clasped His feet and worshiped Him.

POCKETS OF GRACE AUTHORITY

There are places on the earth where the activity of heaven is more evident. Places where it just seems easier to engage with heaven than other places. There are also places that seem to be darker and more spiritually resistant to the things of God.

There is a story recorded in Genesis chapter 28 concerning Jacob. Allow the Lord to reveal what He is saying about pockets of grace authority in the following verses:

Genesis 28:10-19 ESV
(10) Jacob left Beersheba and went toward Haran.

ZION IS COMING

(11) And he came to a certain place and stayed there that night, because the sun had set. Taking one of the stones of the place, he put it under his head and lay down in that place to sleep.

(12) And he dreamed, and behold, there was a ladder set up on the earth, and the top of it reached to heaven. And behold, the angels of God were ascending and descending on it!

(13) And behold, the LORD stood above it and said, "I am the LORD, the God of Abraham your father and the God of Isaac. The land on which you lie I will give to you and to your offspring.

(14) Your offspring shall be like the dust of the earth, and you shall spread abroad to the west and to the east and to the north and to the south, and in you and your offspring shall all the families of the earth be blessed.

(15) Behold, I am with you and will keep you wherever you go, and will bring you back to this land. For I will not leave you until I have done what I have promised you."

(16) Then Jacob awoke from his sleep and said, "Surely the LORD is in this place, and I did not know it."

(17) And he was afraid and said, "How awesome is this place! This is none other than the house of God, and this is the gate of heaven."

(18) So early in the morning Jacob took the stone that he had put under his head and set it up for a pillar and poured oil on the top of it.

(19) He called the name of that place Bethel, but the name of the city was Luz at the first.

These pockets of grace authority will be places similar to Bethel where Jacob encountered an open heaven. The veil separating the natural and the heavenly realm will continue to get thinner.

Resistance from demonic forces will not have effect in these places. Zion is coming to various places in these exciting days!

The rule of God and the rod of His strength will be intense and tangible in these places (see Psalms 110:2). These places will be remarkable because God is coming to rule through His people.

Deliverance and healing will flow like raging waterfalls. Miracles and signs will happen that are so astonishing people will fall to the ground and shout in amazement. God's people will receive free flowing revelation, impartation, and anointing in these places.

God will manifest His tangible fire and glory. God will tabernacle with His people.

The King and His dominion is coming to the earth. He will rule in the midst of His enemies through His people (see Psalms 110).

Allow the Holy Spirit to reveal these truths in the following verses.

> **Isaiah 4:2-6 AMPC**
> (2) In that day the Branch of the Lord shall be beautiful and glorious, and the fruit of the land shall be excellent and lovely to those of Israel who have escaped.
>
> (3) And he who is left in Zion and remains in Jerusalem will be called holy, everyone who is recorded for life in Jerusalem and for eternal life,
>
> (4) After the Lord has washed away the [moral] filth of the daughters of Zion [pride, vanity, haughtiness] and has purged the bloodstains of Jerusalem from the midst of it by the spirit and blast of judgment and by the spirit and blast of burning and sifting.
>
> (5) And the Lord will create over the whole site,

over every dwelling place of Mount Zion and over her assemblies, a cloud and smoke by day and the shining of a flaming fire by night; for over all the glory shall be a canopy (a defense of divine love and protection).

(6) And there shall be a pavilion for shade in the daytime from the heat, and for a place of refuge and a shelter from storm and from rain.

Isaiah 25:3-10 NKJV
(3) Therefore the strong people will glorify You; The city of the terrible nations will fear You.

(4) For You have been a strength to the poor, A strength to the needy in his distress, A refuge from the storm, A shade from the heat; For the blast of the terrible ones is as a storm against the wall.

(5) You will reduce the noise of aliens, As heat in a dry place; As heat in the shadow of a cloud, The song of the terrible ones will be diminished.

(6) And in this mountain The LORD of hosts will make for all people A feast of choice pieces, A feast of wines on the lees, Of fat things full of marrow, Of well-refined wines on the lees.

(7) And He will destroy on this mountain The

surface of the covering cast over all people, And the veil that is spread over all nations.

(8) He will swallow up death forever, And the Lord GOD will wipe away tears from all faces; The rebuke of His people He will take away from all the earth; For the LORD has spoken.

(9) And it will be said in that day: "Behold, this is our God; We have waited for Him, and He will save us. This is the LORD; We have waited for Him; We will be glad and rejoice in His salvation."

(10) For on this mountain the hand of the LORD will rest, And Moab shall be trampled down under Him, As straw is trampled down for the refuse heap.

Zechariah 9:14 AMPC
And the Lord shall be seen over them and His arrow shall go forth as the lightning, and the Lord God will blow the trumpet and will go forth in the windstorms of the south.

Isaiah 60:1-3 AMPC
(1) ARISE [from the depression and prostration in which circumstances have kept you--rise to a new life]! Shine (be radiant with the glory of the Lord), for your light has

come, and the glory of the Lord has risen upon you!

(2) For behold, darkness shall cover the earth, and dense darkness [all] peoples, but the Lord shall arise upon you [O Jerusalem], and His glory shall be seen on you.

(3) And nations shall come to your light, and kings to the brightness of your rising.

God is going to manifest His Glory until the entire earth is filled and everyone sees Him.

Numbers 14:20-21 AMPC
(20) And the Lord said, I have pardoned according to your word.

(21) But truly as I live and as all the earth shall be filled with the glory of the Lord...

Habakkuk 2:14 AMPC
(14) But [the time is coming when] the earth shall be filled with the knowledge of the glory of the Lord as the waters cover the sea.

Matthew 3:11 AMPC
I indeed baptize you in (with) water because of repentance [that is, because of your changing

your minds for the better, heartily amending your ways, with abhorrence of your past sins]. But He Who is coming after me is mightier than I, Whose sandals I am not worthy or fit to take off or carry; He will baptize you with the Holy Spirit and with fire.

Luke 12:49 AMPC
I have come to cast fire upon the earth, and how I wish that it were already kindled!

9
RULE OR BE RULED

Just before daybreak on Yom Kippur morning I heard the Lord say,

"Learn to rule or be ruled by the evil forces trying to come over the land and against My Kingdom.

I will place levels of refuge throughout this nation. A place (places) to escape harm for what is to come.

I am your refuge. In Me they may be safe. These places will be self-identifiable by My Glory Present."

I had the following vision:

I saw a herd of large elephants with long tusks running wildly like a stampede. They were in tight formation and had expressions of fierce determination on their faces. The tusks seem to stand out in the vision.

After this I prayed and asked the Lord what the meaning of the vision meant. Elephants have no rival in power and strength. The elephants were in unity in place and determination. The elephants were moving with purpose.

I was directed to the following scriptures that spoke of ivory. Elephant tusks historically provided the valuable commodity of ivory. 1 Kings 10:18-20 describes the throne that King Solomon made and placed in the Hall of Judgment located in his palace (see 1 Kings 7:7).

1 Kings 10:18-20 NKJV

(18) Moreover the king made a great throne of ivory, and overlaid it with pure gold.

(19) The throne had six steps, and the top of the throne was round at the back; there were armrests on either side of the place of the seat, and two lions stood beside the armrests.

> (20) Twelve lions stood there, one on each side of the six steps; nothing like this had been made for any other kingdom.

The elephant tusks pointed to this great throne of ivory that King Solomon made. The ivory distinguished the throne from all other thrones. Ivory was a highly sought after item that signified the power and strength of the elephant.

The ivory was overlaid with pure gold. Gold is prophetic of the glory of God.

There were six steps leading up to the throne. Six represents the day God created man. The seat of the throne was the seventh level beyond the steps. Seven means completion and points to the Sabbath or rest of God.

Take note that, "nothing like this had been made for any other kingdom" (see verse 20).

The power and authority offered to God's people comes from the rest He offers them. The rest of the Lord means that we have ceased from our own works by allowing His Presence to be our life (see Hebrews 4:10). God's rest is always tied to His Presence (see Exodus 33:14).

Hebrews 4:10 NKJV
For he who has entered His rest has himself also ceased from his works as God did from His.

Exodus 33:14 NKJV
And He said, "My Presence will go with you, and I will give you rest."

Matthew 11:28 NKJV
Come to Me, all you who labor and are heavy laden, and I will give you rest.

The two lions at each arm rest represent the law and the Spirit. This is alluding to the Transfiguration of Jesus when Moses and Elijah appeared to visit with Him (see Matthew 17:1-6).

The twelve lions that stood on each side of the six steps are symbolic of the twelve tribes of Israel and the twelve founding apostles. Twelve is prophetic of God's government.

God is establishing His kingdom on the earth. And Jesus is ruling in the midst of His enemies on earth while being seated at the right hand of the Father in the heavenly Zion. Jesus is seated at the right hand of the Father UNTIL all their enemies have been made

His footstool (see Psalms 110:1).

> **Psalms 110:1-3 ESV**
> (1) A Psalm of David. The LORD says to my Lord: "Sit at my right hand, until I make your enemies your footstool."
>
> (2) The LORD sends forth from Zion your mighty scepter. Rule in the midst of your enemies!
>
> (3) Your people will offer themselves freely on the day of your power, in holy garments; from the womb of the morning, the dew of your youth will be yours.

> **Hebrews 10:12-14 WEB**
> (12) but he, when he had offered one sacrifice for sins forever, sat down on the right hand of God;
>
> (13) from that time waiting until his enemies are made the footstool of his feet.
>
> (14) For by one offering he has perfected forever those who are being sanctified.

He is ruling over His enemies by sending the rod of His strength which is His Spirit. He is sending His powerful Holy Spirit and working through and upon

His people on the earth (see Psalms 110).

Jesus is King of kings and Lord of lords. Jesus is ruler over the kings of the earth. He has made us kings and priests to His God (see Revelations 1:4-6). Consider the following verses and allow the Holy Spirit to reveal the truth that we are kings and lords that Jesus rules through.

Deuteronomy 10:15-18 ESV
(15) Yet the LORD set his heart in love on your fathers and chose their offspring after them, you above all peoples, as you are this day.

(16) Circumcise therefore the foreskin of your heart, and be no longer stubborn.

(17) For the LORD your God is God of gods and Lord of lords, the great, the mighty, and the awesome God, who is not partial and takes no bribe.

(18) He executes justice for the fatherless and the widow, and loves the sojourner, giving him food and clothing.

Psalms 136:1-3 ESV
(1) Give thanks to the LORD, for he is good, for his steadfast love endures forever.

(2) Give thanks to the God of gods, for his steadfast love endures forever.

(3) Give thanks to the Lord of lords, for his steadfast love endures forever;

Daniel 2:46-48 ESV
(46) Then King Nebuchadnezzar fell upon his face and paid homage to Daniel, and commanded that an offering and incense be offered up to him.

(47) The king answered and said to Daniel, "Truly, your God is God of gods and Lord of kings, and a revealer of mysteries, for you have been able to reveal this mystery."

(48) Then the king gave Daniel high honors and many great gifts, and made him ruler over the whole province of Babylon and chief prefect over all the wise men of Babylon.

Revelation 1:4-6 NKJV
(4) John, to the seven churches which are in Asia: Grace to you and peace from Him who is and who was and who is to come, and from the seven Spirits who are before His throne,

(5) and from Jesus Christ, the faithful witness, the firstborn from the dead, and the ruler

over the kings of the earth. To Him who loved us and washed us from our sins in His own blood,

(6) and has made us kings and priests to His God and Father, to Him be glory and dominion forever and ever. Amen.

Revelation 17:13-14 NKJV

(13) These are of one mind, and they will give their power and authority to the beast.

(14) These will make war with the Lamb, and the Lamb will overcome them, for He is Lord of lords and King of kings; and those who are with Him are called, chosen, and faithful."

Revelation 19:11-16 NKJV

(11) Now I saw heaven opened, and behold, a white horse. And He who sat on him was called Faithful and True, and in righteousness He judges and makes war.

(12) His eyes were like a flame of fire, and on His head were many crowns. He had a name written that no one knew except Himself.

(13) He was clothed with a robe dipped in blood, and His name is called The Word of God.

(14) And the armies in heaven, clothed in fine linen, white and clean, followed Him on white horses.

(15) Now out of His mouth goes a sharp sword, that with it He should strike the nations. And He Himself will rule them with a rod of iron. He Himself treads the winepress of the fierceness and wrath of Almighty God.

(16) And He has on His robe and on His thigh a name written: KING OF KINGS AND LORD OF LORDS.

I heard the Lord say, "*Learn to rule or be ruled by the evil forces trying to come over the land and against My Kingdom.*"

We must awaken to our Lord's plan to take over the kingdoms of the earth through us. This means that our assignment is to rescue all people from the demonic control of wickedness in every area of society. God loves the whole world and He doesn't want anyone to perish. His goal is to bring many sons to glory (see Hebrews 2:10). He is going to conform us to His image by His Spirit (see 2 Corinthians 3:17-18).

RULE OR BE RULED

2 Corinthians 3:17-18 WEB
(17) Now the Lord is the Spirit and where the Spirit of the Lord is, there is liberty.

(18) But we all, with unveiled face seeing the glory of the Lord as in a mirror, are transformed into the same image from glory to glory, even as from the Lord, the Spirit.

All of creation is waiting on us to come forward.

Romans 8:19 ESV
For the creation waits with eager longing for the revealing of the sons of God.

There is a coming generation of people that will be like Jesus. They will have gotten back everything Adam lost. There is no reason that we cannot be that generation. In fact God is calling for it NOW.

A key to becoming what He wants us to be is to see Him as "He is" (see 1 John 3:2). Many people worship the One who was or look forward to the One who is to come. These are amazing, but we must also see Him as "He is."

1 John 3:1-2 NKJV
(1) Behold what manner of love the Father has bestowed on us, that we should be called children of God! Therefore the world does not

know us, because it did not know Him.

(2) Beloved, now we are children of God; and it has not yet been revealed what we shall be, but we know that when He is revealed, we shall be like Him, for we shall see Him as He is.

We must ask God to reveal religious veils that keep us from seeing Him as He is. We must repent of unbelief and come to His word as children and believe.

Jesus stirred up the religious rulers by quoting a Psalm where God called His people gods. Jesus said that the Father called His people gods (see John 10:35)!

John 10:33-36 NKJV
(33) The Jews answered Him, saying, "For a good work we do not stone You, but for blasphemy, and because You, being a Man, make Yourself God."

(34) Jesus answered them, "Is it not written in your law, 'I SAID, "YOU ARE GODS" '?

(35) If He called them gods, to whom the word of God came (and the Scripture cannot be broken),

(36) do you say of Him whom the Father sanctified and sent into the world, 'You are blaspheming,' because I said, 'I am the Son of God'?

They accused Jesus of being a man that was trying to be God. The truth is, He being God made Himself a man so we would become gods. This speaks to the degree that God wants to delegate His power and authority to us.

Jesus was quoting from Psalms chapter 82. This Psalm says that God stands in the congregation of the mighty and He judges among the gods. That is God ruling in our midst by His Spirit (see Psalms 82:1).

Then the Holy Spirit, through the Psalmist, issued an indictment to God's people for not living up to His aspirations for them. Some of the things they were to do were:

- **Defend the poor and fatherless.**
- **Do justice to the afflicted and needy.**
- **Deliver the poor and needy.**
- **Free them from the wicked.**

They were to be like gods on the earth reflecting their Father by ruling and reigning over the enemies of God. God said, "You are gods, And all of you are children of the Most High" (see Psalms 82:6).

They refused the high calling of God and so the Psalmist said they would die like men or one of the princes of a conquered people.

> **Psalms 82:1-8 NKJV**
> (1) A Psalm of Asaph. God stands in the congregation of the mighty; He judges among the gods.
>
> (2) How long will you judge unjustly, And show partiality to the wicked? Selah
>
> (3) Defend the poor and fatherless; Do justice to the afflicted and needy.
>
> (4) Deliver the poor and needy; Free them from the hand of the wicked.
>
> (5) They do not know, nor do they understand; They walk about in darkness; All the foundations of the earth are unstable.
>
> (6) I said, "You are gods, And all of you are children of the Most High.
>
> (7) But you shall die like men, And fall like one of the princes."
>
> (8) Arise, O God, judge the earth; For You shall inherit all nations.

The devil is using the same old tactics today to keep God's people from His highest calling. It's the same weapon that he used against Adam and Eve in the garden of Eden before they fell.

In the garden the devil began to question what God had told Adam and Eve and to place doubts into them. The serpent started with Eve by telling her that God doesn't want them to eat from the Tree of the Knowledge of Good and Evil because He doesn't want them to be "like God" (see Genesis 3:5).

The truth is Adam and Eve were already like God. They had been created in His image. They were His children. They had dominion over everything created on the earth, including the devil.

The only weapon that could hurt Adam and Eve was the lie or unbelief in what God had said. Once they ate from the forbidden tree their eyes were open and they had knowledge of sin.

Therefore, they became accountable for what they knew but they were now separated from God. Because they were separated from God they didn't have the ability to live up to the knowledge they possessed (see Luke 12:48). The knowledge of right or wrong was a form of the law. And when the law entered in then sin entered in (see Romans 5:13).

RULE OR BE RULED

Genesis 3:1-5 ESV

(1) Now the serpent was more crafty than any other beast of the field that the LORD God had made. He said to the woman, "Did God actually say, 'You shall not eat of any tree in the garden'?"

(2) And the woman said to the serpent, "We may eat of the fruit of the trees in the garden,

(3) but God said, 'You shall not eat of the fruit of the tree that is in the midst of the garden, neither shall you touch it, lest you die.'"

(4) But the serpent said to the woman, "You will not surely die.

(5) For God knows that when you eat of it your eyes will be opened, and you will be like God, knowing good and evil."

We must awaken to what our Father has said about us today. We must look at His word with childlike faith so that we can recognize the lies of the devil.

The devil says, "God doesn't want you to be like Him." The Bible says that He does (see 2 Corinthians 3:18)!

The devil says, "Who do you think you are? You're trying be like God." The Bible says that it was God's original intent for us (see Genesis 1:26)!

The devil says, "Watch out that's New Age teaching!" The devil has always copied what God is doing and then perverts it to drive God's people away from the real thing (see Luke 11:13).

We must accept the Lord's call to rule by submitting to His Holy Spirit. We can't afford to continue as we have in the past. The land is being overrun by demonic forces whose designs are to kill, steal, and destroy.

We will accept the Lord's offer and enter into His rest by ceasing from our own works so that His works will appear through us by the powerful Person of the Holy Spirit.

Exodus 7:1-2 NKJV
(1) So the LORD said to Moses: "See, I have made you as God to Pharaoh, and Aaron your brother shall be your prophet.

(2) You shall speak all that I command you. And Aaron your brother shall tell Pharaoh to send the children of Israel out of his land.

I heard the Lord say, "*I will place levels of refuge throughout this nation. A place (places) to escape harm for what is to come. I am your refuge. In Me they may be safe. These places will be self-identifiable by My Glory Present.*"

RULE OR BE RULED

God will establish His Presence on the earth as we fully yield to Him and allow Him to rule through us. There will be places that will function like embassies of His kingdom in the spirit realm.

> **Proverbs 13:17 NKJV**
> A wicked messenger falls into trouble, But a faithful ambassador brings health.

> **2 Corinthians 5:20 ESV**
> Therefore, we are ambassadors for Christ, God making his appeal through us. We implore you on behalf of Christ, be reconciled to God.

God's people will learn the power of their words, the power of unity, and the power of imagination. Nothing will be withheld from them with God. He will build for Himself a place to dwell using living stones with Jesus being the chief cornerstone. This tower is intended to reach heaven and make a name for our King.

> **Genesis 4:6-7 NKJV**
> (6) So the LORD said to Cain, "Why are you angry? And why has your countenance fallen?

(7) If you do well, will you not be accepted? And if you do not do well, sin lies at the door. And its desire is for you, but you should rule over it."

Romans 5:17 NKJV
For if by the one man's offense death reigned through the one, much more those who receive abundance of grace and of the gift of righteousness will reign in life through the One, Jesus Christ.)

FINAL WORD

I heard the Lord say,
"I am exposing evil and
wickedness at all levels of
the US government.

I am calling for righteousness
to rule the land again."

FINAL WORD

God will continue to expose wickedness and corruption in city, county, state, and federal government in the United States. God has good plans for the United States! And we will once again be 'one nation under God with liberty and justice for all.'

Our King Jesus is raising up a people that will rule over wickedness in order to establish His righteousness in the earth.

God's people must accept His call to rule. This will happen as we believe and follow Him.

LASTING LIBERTY
MINISTRIES

For more information or
for prayer requests
visit us at *lastingliberty.org*

LASTING LIBERTY MINISTRIES
PO BOX #141913
3900 Teleport Blvd
Irving, TX 75014

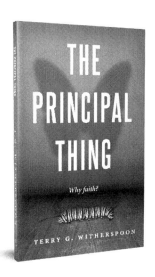

CHECK OUT TERRY'S OTHER BOOKS!

THE PRINCIPAL THING: WHY FAITH?

You can live a life without natural limitations.

Most books written about faith deal with the "what" and the "how," but *The Principal Thing* primarily answers the question of "why." The answers reveal the value and relevance of faith today and God's plan for mankind.

Written simply and directly, *The Principal Thing* can be easily read and understood by everyone. Each chapter is highlighted by supernatural events in the lives of everyday people. You will be drawn from one chapter to the next while growing in affection for your own faith and the God who provided it.

"Your life will be significantly blessed and enriched greatly by not only reading this book but truly studying and applying its teaching to your life... take your time as you read and ponder the principles of this timely book." – **Bobby Conner, Eagles View Ministries**

AVAILABLE ON KINDLE, PAPERBACK, AND AUDIOBOOK ON AMAZON & AUDIBLE!

Made in the USA
Columbia, SC
21 February 2021